Coachella Valley

Images of Nature

**Photographs and Text by
James W. Cornett**

Cover photograph:
Brittlebush (*Encelia farinosa*), near Indian Canyons Tribal Park
Photograph taken March 25, 2011

Page 1 photograph:
Whipple Yucca (*Hesperoyucca whipplei*) and Mount San Jacinto.
Photograph taken May, 1991

Page 2 photograph:
Lower Palm Canyon, Indian Canyons Tribal Park
Photograph taken October 31, 2005

Title page photograph:
Male Costa's Hummingbird, *Calypte costae*

Canterbury Bells
Phacelia campanularia

Contents Page Photograph:
Kit Fox, *Vulpes macrotis*

Published by
nature trails press
P.O. Box 846
Palm Springs, California 92263
Telephone 760-320-2664
www.naturetrailspress.com

Contents

Introduction

I first visited the Coachella Valley in 1965 while still in high school. Having just received a driver's license, I coerced my parents into letting me borrow the older of two family cars. I was ecstatic when they told me the vehicle could be used for the entire Easter vacation.

My friend Rob and I grabbed everything we needed and drove to the desert, two hours east of our homes in Los Angeles. Passing the city of Beaumont and entering the San Gorgonio Pass, we encountered the vertical escarpment of Mount San Jacinto's north face. It was so tall, so sheer. I couldn't remember ever seeing anything like it.

Had it not been for our frugal budget, we would have taken Tramway Road to the Palm Springs Aerial Tramway. Riding upwards nearly 8,000 feet above downtown Palm Springs and into the coniferous forest at the top would have been a thrill. Nowhere else in the continental U.S. can one commute so quickly between desert and high mountain forest.

We continued south on Highway 111 through Palm Springs and past throngs of fellow students gathered for holiday reverie. Rob and I were more interested in desert than parties and we headed south to the Indian Canyons. In Palm Canyon both of us were amazed at the enormous number of palms. They seemed out of place in the arid surroundings.

After a short hike we returned to the car and drove to the vast dune field in the center of the valley. Our first Coachella Valley fringe-toed lizard was seen and we followed it to the spot where it dove beneath the sand and disappeared. I shoved my hand into the dune and pulled out a wiggling reptile.

The next day Rob and I drove east to the Mecca Hills and hiked several hours through a maze of slot canyons. We found a desert tortoise that promptly withdrew into its shell as we approached. The tortoise remained tucked away in its bony fortress even as we departed to resume hiking up the canyon.

Years before Rob and I made our trip, my family had visited the Salton Sea. We camped on the shoreline and used our boat to ski and fish. Wanting to revisit the site, Rob and I drove the short distance to the Sea. As we stood on the shoreline and gazed across the water, neither of us was aware that we were viewing the largest lake in California.

The next day we traveled to Highway 74, locally known as Palms to Pines Highway. The morning was spent hiking in the Santa Rosa Mountains. It was here I found my first blooming beavertail cactus. Both of us wondered how such an unimpressive plant could produce such spectacular flowers. As we returned down the canyon, a bighorn ram leaped from the wash bottom and moved effortlessly up the canyon wall, directly in front of us. At the rim it stopped and stared back before trotting out of sight.

When I reflect on these first experiences I am continually amazed. In spite of dramatic growth in the area's population over the past half century most of the Valley's wondrous places are still intact, beautiful and accessible to all.

The image collection contained in these pages represents more than forty years of photographing local landscapes, plants and animals. I have selected images that represent diversity, both of environments and life forms, and have organized them according to habitat types: valley floor, washes, alluvial fans, oases, canyons, mountains and the Salton Sea. Cahuilla Indian presence, prior to contact with Europeans, is also included.

I hope viewing these images will begin (or renew) an interest in experiencing and preserving the natural heritage that is such a dramatic aspect of the Coachella Valley. Much land has already been protected as the valley is surrounded by four state parks, a national park, two tribal parks, a national monument and several private preserves. The Coachella Valley Multiple Species Habitat Conservation Plan established nearly two dozen additional conservation areas. No other place in the world is so well protected. I encourage everyone to venture out and experience these special places in our extraordinary Coachella Valley.

Looking north into Coachella Valley from Vista Point, Highway 74. Photograph taken January 6, 2008.

Wind, Sand, Valley Floor

Sand Verbena (Abronia villosa) *in foreground
and Desert Sunflower* (Geraea canescens)
*in background; Edom Hill, Cathedral City.
Photograph taken March 23, 2005.*

More than anything else, the surface of the central valley floor has been shaped by wind.

As the Coachella Valley heats up in spring, hot air rises and creates a vacuum that sucks in cool air from coastal Southern California. Ocean breezes accelerate to gale force as winds funnel through the narrow, San Gorgonio pass located at the valley's west end.

For at least five million years, massive amounts of sand have piled up at the mouth of the pass. The sand is alluvial runoff originating in the San Bernardino and San Jacinto mountains.

The result of these phenomena has been the blanketing of the valley floor with sand carried eastward by frequent and powerful winds. Prior to the arrival of Europeans late in the 18th century, vast dunes and mesquite-topped sand hummocks stretched from what is now Palm Springs all the way to Indio and La Quinta. Today, the vast majority of this dunescape lies beneath homes, shopping malls and golf courses.

Dune primrose, Oenothera deltoides, *was once common on dunes. Today it competes with exotic Sahara mustard,* Brassica tournefortii.

Dunescapes, such as this one near Washington Street and Avenue 48, once enveloped mountain bases from Palm Springs to La Quinta. Photograph taken December, 1998.

Active dunes fields can still be observed between the town of Thousand Palms and Washington Street, north of Interstate 10.

Sand storm on the Whitewater River Floodplain.
Photograph taken April, 1978.

Most blowsand originates in the San Gorgonio Pass where drainages from the San Bernardino and San Jacinto mountains spread out onto the valley floor. The largest alluvial flows emanate from Whitewater Canyon near the junction of Highway 111 and Interstate 10, a point where spring winds reach their greatest velocity.

Sand carried down valley (to the southeast) by wind provides a near perfect medium for ephemeral wildflowers. Surfaces are buried in blowsand in late spring and early summer of the previous year leaving little or no competition. Late fall and winter rains (when they occur) germinate buried seeds that have no difficulty establishing roots in loose sand.

In years of above-average winter precipitation, spring blooms can be spectacular. Prior to the widespread establishment of an introduced weed known as the Sahara Mustard (*Brassica tournefortii*) in the 1990s, massive blooms of the hairy sand verbena (*Abronia villosa*) made the Coachella Valley appear pink in satellite photographs.

Sand Verbena was the most common wildflower on the valley floor. Recently, it has been replaced by the exotic Sahara Mustard.

Hairy Sand-Verbena covers the loose, windblown sand of the valley floor.

The federally endangered Coachella Valley Milkvetch (Astragalus lentiginosus coachellae) thrives where deposits of windblown sand exist. Photograph taken on April 1, 2011.

The abrasive power of wind-carried sand can be frighteningly destructive. An unusually severe windstorm struck the Coachella Valley in June of 1979. Scores of drivers were forced to abandon their cars along Indian Avenue when visibility dropped to zero. The next day stranded automobiles were found to have had their windows blasted away and paint sanded off. The entire windward side of each vehicle was transformed into a shiny metal surface.

Through much of the Coachella Valley the lower portions of wooden utility poles must be covered with metal jackets lest they be eaten through by wind-driven sand.

Over decades, the hardest of rocks can be carved and polished by blowsand.

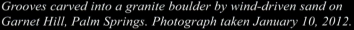

Grooves carved into a granite boulder by wind-driven sand on Garnet Hill, Palm Springs. Photograph taken January 10, 2012.

Opposite Page: Polished, fluted and grooved rocks created by decades of recurring sand storms. Photograph taken January 8, 2008, near intersection of Gene Autry Trail and I-10.

The ocean of dunes and hummocks that once covered the Coachella Valley remained isolated from other dune systems for thousands of years. As a result, many of the dune-adapted plants and animals evolved into new species or subspecies. These taxa have a different appearance when compared with their close relatives living elsewhere in the deserts of California.

The Coachella Valley Fringe-toed Lizard is an example of this speciation. Though two other fringe-toed lizard species occur in California, only the species in the photograph to the right (*Uma inornata*) is found in the Coachella Valley. Thirty-three miles to the south of the valley lives the Colorado Desert Fringe-toed Lizard (*Uma notata*) and twenty-six miles to the north-east lives the Mojave Fringe-toed Lizard (*Uma scoparia*).

Fringe-toed lizards derive their name from enlarged scales on the toes of their front and hind feet. The scales increase traction on the loose sand on which they run. The image below shows the fringed scales on toes of a fringe-toed lizard.

Front foot of Coachella Valley Fringe-toed Lizard.

The Coachella Valley Fringe-toed Lizard is listed as a threatened species by federal and state governments. It is only found in areas of loose, wind-blown sand in the Coachella Valley.

Each spring and summer powerful winds blast through of the San Gorgonio Pass just north and west of downtown Palm Springs. So pervasive and predictable are the air movements that hundreds of wind-driven, electricity generating turbines have been erected in and near the pass. (A single modern generator produces enough electricity to power four hundred homes for a year.) Although the jury is still out on the negative impact the rotating blades have on birds and bats, terrestrial plants and animals continue to live within a "wind farm." Minimizing grading during construction, prohibiting domestic animals and animal-porous fences are practices that facilitate compatibility between farm and terrestrial desert ecosystems.

Clean and renewable wind resources are an excellent way to produce electricity. The wind resource at the mouth of the San Gorgonio Pass is considered one of the best in the country.

———————————————

Truck toppled by strong winds along Indian Avenue north of Palm Springs. Note steel jacket on bottom of utility poll. Photograph taken June, 1975.

Spring-blooming Desert Dandelions, Malacothrix glabrata, *near the edge of a wind farm north of Palm Springs in the upper Coachella Valley. Photograph taken April 19, 2010.*

Burrowing Owls, Athene cunicularia, *thrive in sandy areas on the valley floor. Photograph taken in the city of Coachella, May 13, 2006.*

Floods, Fans and Bajadas

A Smoke Tree, Psorothamnus spinosus,
*in Palm Canyon Wash. Successive
winter storms can temporarily fill washes.
Photograph taken January 17, 2005.*

The sandy floor of the Coachella Valley is a result of the erosion of rock in the surrounding mountains. Over eons of time, precipitation and runoff grind solid rock into sand and gravel that flow down usually dry desert stream courses or *washes*. Ultimately, this *alluvium* spreads out to form alluvial fans at the mouth of canyons which, in turn, coalesce into *bajadas* just above the sandy valley floor.

In spite of occasional scouring floodwaters, washes are productive environments since they receive both precipitation and runoff. There is often sufficient soil moisture to support trees including ironwood, desert willow, palo verde and smoke trees.

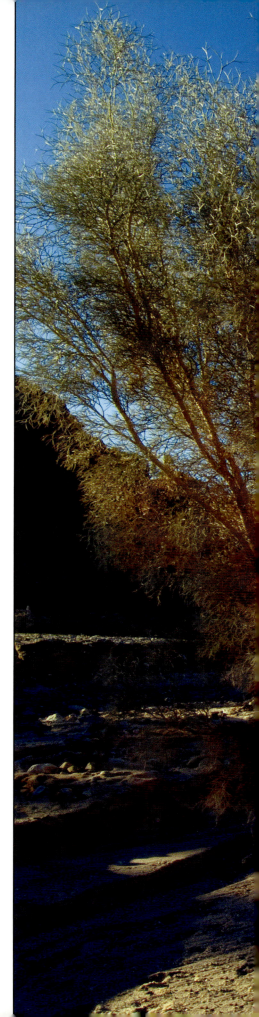

Smoke Trees (Psorothamnus spinosus) *are found in most Coachella Valley washes. Palm Canyon Wash, Palm Springs. Photograph taken January 22, 2011.*

Apricot Mallow (Sphaeralcea ambigua) *and Little San Bernardino Mountains north of city of Coachella. Photograph taken April, 2008.*

Rain in the Coachella Valley occurs primarily in winter. Storms originate in the north and west over the Pacific Ocean. They move slowly across valley skies with precipitation sometimes falling for several hours. Such storms rarely drop more than half an inch of rain.

Rare summer storms, as shown in the photograph to the right, move into the valley from the south. The mechanism that attracts and facilitates summer storms is a thermal low pressure system caused by heat rising from the hot desert floor. This creates a vacuum that draws in moist air from the Gulf of California. On those unusual occasions when such storms reach the Coachella Valley, rainfall is brief but often intense. Every few years an inch or more of precipitation falls in less than an hour. Rainfall can be very localized. Indio may receive an inch and nearby Palm Desert no rain at all.

Because of high evaporation rates and rapid runoff, summer storms are of minimal benefit to plants and animals.

Lightning typically accompanies summer thunderstorms.

Summer storm enters the Coachella Valley from the south. View to the southeast from the base of the Little San Bernardino Mountains.

In years when late fall and winter rainfall is significantly above the long-term average, spring wildflower displays can be spectacular. Unlike the sandy floor of the central valley that has been usurped by exotic weed species such as Sahara mustard (*Brassica tournefortii*), washes and alluvial fans are less impacted by introduced species. The coarser and more compacted soils make the establishment of invasive exotics more difficult and are, therefore, a better place to find native wildflowers. Desert dandelions are one of the most abundant ephemerals and can still cover acre upon acre on bajadas in the western and northern Coachella Valley.

Fremont Pincushion, Chaenactis fremontii, *often grows in association with Desert Dandelion.*

Desert Dandelions, Malacothrix glabrata, *dominate a bajada near the intersection of Palm Drive and Pierson Boulevard, near Desert Hot Springs. Photograph taken March 16, 2005.*

Gambel's quail reach greatest abundance on bajadas and alluvial fans.

My wife and I spend much time in spring counting and recounting Gambel's quail chicks. The number constantly changes. One spring we saw 17 chicks accompanied by a mated pair. A week later the same parents had only 14 chicks. By May 18th, try as I might, I could only come up with 10 chicks. My wife reconfirmed the count. On May 31st the number of chicks had declined to just 8. What happened to the chicks? The pair appeared to be good parents, herding the young together with at least one parent always on guard and the other showing young where to look for seeds. If one youngster lagged behind, mom or dad would immediately go back and return it to the group. If a roadrunner or other predator came too close the adult quail would attack with amazing fury.

We seldom observe chick fatalities but obviously mortality occurs. On one occasion I found a chick that had drowned in a waterhole we created. On another occasion I found a chick being swallowed by a speckled rattlesnake. In coveys that I have monitored, chick attrition is always more than fifty percent. It is the lucky chick that survives and become an adult.

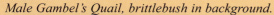

Male Gambel's Quail, brittlebush in background.

A female Gambel's quail (Callipepla gambelii) *watches over her young. Photograph taken May 30, 2009.*

Winter storm passes over the Little San Bernardino Mountains north of Desert Hot Springs, California Barrel Cacti (Ferocactus cylindraceus) are in foreground. Photograph taken February 10, 2010.

The chuparosa, known to botanists as *Justicia californica*, reaches its greatest abundance along wash margins and on alluvial fans where plants receive both precipitation and runoff from nearby mountains.

There are not many plant species in the desert that produce red flowers. Perhaps that is why the chuparosa shrub is popular among residents and tourists—it's something different, something unexpected. That chuparosa begins flowering in winter, when the Valley's human population reaches its zenith, no doubt enhances the plant's notoriety.

Chuparosa is the Spanish word for hummingbird. The common name is appropriate. Hummingbirds regularly visit chuparosa flowers to sip sugary nectar that is abundant inside the blossoms. In fact, each flower is so long and tubular that only the hummingbird, with its extended bill and tongue, can successfully reach the nectar.

California Fuchsia, (Epilobium canum), another hummingbird favorite, blooms in fall. Fuchsia plants are smaller and much less common than Chuparosa.

Chuparosa in bloom just north of Indian Canyons Tribal Park. Photograph taken March 25, 2011.

*Mission Creek Wash filled with
runoff water from a winter storm.
Photograph taken February 1, 2005.*

The Coachella Valley's largest terrestrial reptile has been declared a threatened species by both state and federal governments. The introduction of exotic diseases, indiscriminate off-road-vehicle use, habitat loss and illegal collecting are the main reasons for its increasing scarcity.

Though once considered absent from the Coachella Valley, intensive searching has revealed desert tortoises are widespread in the valley. Individuals have been found on the Chino Cone in Palm Springs and west and east of Desert Hot Springs. An unusually dense population exists just west of Whitewater Canyon.

Female Desert Tortoise in burrow on Chino Cone, Palm Springs. Photograph taken June 2, 2008.

An adult Desert Tortoise in field of blooming Hairy Sand-Verbena. Photograph taken March 13, 2009.

Flooded Whitewater River Channel during successive winter storms.
Photograph taken along Gene Autry Trail, January 21, 2010.

The western end of the Coachella Valley, at the mouth of the San Gorgonio Pass north of Palm Springs, receives the greatest precipitation. In an average year rainfall totals approximately six inches with most rain falling in winter. Conversely, the eastern end of the Valley receives only half that much.

In years of unusually high winter rainfall road washouts are frequent. This is expected, particularly in the upper or western end of the Valley as it lies close to the tallest mountains and the largest watershed. The upper valley also receives the greatest amount of winter precipitation.

Snow Creek Road may wash out during winter storms. Photograph taken January 19, 2005.

Winter runoff heading down the San Gorgonio Wash and into the Coachella Valley. Photograph taken January 19, 2005.

*Summer flood path from the Mecca
Hills at southeastern end of the
Coachella Valley. Photograph taken
January 1, 2012*

There are at least twenty species of cacti that occur in the Coachella Valley region. All are restricted in their distribution to the coarse, well-drained soils of bajadas, alluvial fans, canyons and hillsides. With a diameter of up to twenty-four inches and a height sometimes in excess of five feet, the California Barrel Cactus, *Ferocactus cylindraceus,* is the largest cactus in the region. As a group, Coachella Valley cacti begin flowering in late March. Blooming peaks in April but continues into June in the surrounding mountains.

Cacti are rarely found in washes. Their shallow roots do not provide the anchorage necessary to remain in place during floods.

Cacti, such as the California Barrel Cactus, are common on the upper portions of alluvial fans. Snow-capped Mount San Jacinto in background. Photograph taken April, 1999.

Colony of Teddy-Bear Cholla, Opuntia bigelovii, *near the base of the Little San Bernardino Mountains, Sky Valley. Photograph taken January 20, 2012.*

Palms and Oases

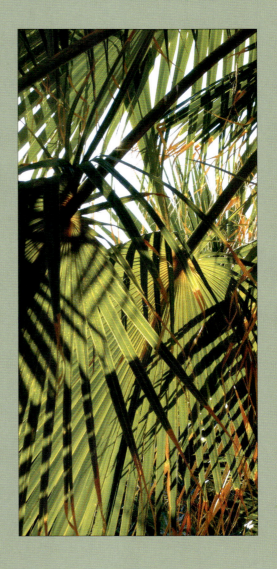

Palm Canyon,
Indian Canyons Tribal Park,
south of downtown Palm Springs.
Photograph taken October 31, 2005.

Most of the Coachella Valley is a hyper-arid region and one of the driest places in North America. Consider that the city of Coachella receives a mere 3.53 inches of precipitation in an entire year. Palm Desert receives even less, just 3.15 inches; Indio lesser still at 3.05 inches. The impact of this aridity is made more intense by very hot summers. Indio has an *average* daily maximum temperature in July (the hottest month) of 107° Fahrenheit. Palm Springs is even hotter at 108°. Mecca beats all desert communities with an average temperature in July of 109°.

With such intense heat and so little moisture, there is little water for plants, animals or humans. Without water, life cannot exist. Thus, it is small wonder that a first impression of the desert is often one of desolation. To lost and thirsty prospectors of bygone days, the stark landscape must have seemed endless.

From this perspective, the Coachella Valley would be the last place where one would expect to find dense groves of water-loving palm trees. Yet such groves exist complete with shade, cooler temperatures and, above all, life-giving water. At the heart of the oasis is the most massive palm in North America, the desert fan palm, *Washingtonia filifera.* In the Coachella Valley there are approximately 12,000 wild adult palms contained in dozens of oases.

The hanging fruit clusters of the desert fan palm mature in fall.

Beyond the barrel cacti and yellow-flowered brittlebush are desert fan palms, Washingtonia filifera, *growing along the bottom of Palm Canyon in the Indian Canyons Tribal Park. Photograph taken March 8, 2008.*

59

Randall Henderson was the late editor and publisher of a wonderful monthly publication known as *Desert Magazine*. Henderson possessed a profound affection for palm oasis environments. His personal quest was to visit every oasis of which he became aware, an effort that lasted most of his adult life. During Henderson's tenure at *Desert Magazine* he often wrote about oasis visits including precise directions on how to locate them. He carried a mechanical counter to record the exact number of palms. The counts became the basis for later ecological research.

Henderson is remembered with two palm oases named after him: Henderson Palms in Palm Springs, California, and Randall Palms near Anza-Borrego Desert State Park. Anyone interested in the desert Southwest or palm oases should visit a local library and read some of Henderson's *Desert Magazine* articles. His words can also be found in two of his books: *Sun, Sand and Solitude* and *On Desert Trails*.

American robin on hanging fruit stalk of a desert fan palm. Palm fruits are in important winter food resource for robins.

The shaded, moist floor of Pushawalla Palms lies along the San Andreas Fault. This canyon palm oasis lies in the center of the Coachella Valley just west and north of the community of Thousand Palms. Photograph taken March 7, 2007.

The desert fan palm is one of the tallest plants native to the Sonoran Desert and, by weight, the largest palm in North America. Mature trees are known to reach eighty feet in height and attain a trunk diameter approaching four feet. The desert fan palm is also one of the few palms whose dead leaves remain affixed to the trunk to form a smooth shag often referred to as a skirt or petticoat.

Considered a fast-growing species, a typical desert fan palm adds about one foot of trunk height per year. This growth rate is maintained for approximately the first twenty years. After that, the growth rate steadily decreases. Trees over fifty feet in height grow very slowly, probably not more than one to two inches per year. At sites where water supplies are seasonally restricted, or where climate conditions are relatively cold, young palms may grow just two or three inches each year.

The most rapid growth rate I have recorded is at Thousand Palms Oasis near the community of Thousand Palms. A tree there developed a ten-foot-tall trunk in six years. It grew in the shade of numerous other palms and had germinated in a warm spring. These two factors were thought to be the causes of its rapid growth.

Normally, the "bark" of the palm trunk is obscured by the dead leaves that form the unique shag of desert fan palms. The bark is exposed only if the shag is burned away by fire (which the palm usually survives) or, in very rare instances, when all or part of the shag is blown off by severe winds.

The tallest and densest stand of desert fan palms in the world is located in Palm Canyon's main grove located in the Indian Canyons Tribal Park. Photograph taken December 16, 2007.

Desert fan palms are not adapted to the aridity that characterizes the Coachella Valley. Their ability to survive in the desert environment is intimately associated with a specialized distribution. Desert fan palms are only found where water is permanently at or near the surface—at desert springs, seeps and streams.

Places where water flows on the desert's surface are obviously rare. In the Coachella Valley, however, there are two features that result in an unusual number of springs and oases. The most famous is the San Andreas Fault that cuts through the middle of the valley. Along the fault, water flowing downhill and beneath the surface is impounded. The impounded water rises to the surface at numerous locations. Birds and coyotes disperse palm seeds from existing palm oases to new springs and seeps.

As its name suggests, the Coachella Valley is surrounded by mountains. Mountains capture more precipitation than valleys. Most of the water runs off quickly down canyons but much is released more slowly through fractures in rock. Large mountain masses, like the San Jacinto Mountains behind Palm Springs, collect sufficient precipitation and release it so slowly that large canyons may contain surface flows year round.

Andreas Canyon in the Indian Canyons Tribal Park drains such a large portion of the San Jacinto Mountains that is supports year-round surface flows. Photograph taken April, 1988.

Though palms have been around for millions of years, the desert fan palm is most likely a recently evolved, invasive species. Nevertheless, for more than half a century this local palm tree was said to be a *relict species*, a species widespread in the remote past but now surviving in a few isolated desert oases. In 1966, scientists said it was endangered, its populations threatened and its numbers declining.

More recently scientists have discovered the precise opposite. The range of the desert fan palm is expanding as it invades new springs and waterholes. In addition, numbers have doubled in the wild in less than a century—from 15,000 wild palms before World War II to over 35,000 in the current century. At Willis Palms, near the town of Thousand Palms, numbers jumped from 370 adult palms in 1983 to 612 in the late 1990s, a whopping 65% increase. Throughout the Coachella Valley and the entire American Southwest, desert fan palms are thriving. Global warming tends to favor plant species whose lineage originates in the tropics. This human-caused phenomenon is the most likely reason for the expanding numbers and distribution of the desert fan palm.

Stems of palm fronds, called petioles, are covered with sharp, brittle spines on palms less than twenty-six feet in height.

Aging palm fronds at Willis Palms located in the Coachella Valley Preserve, near the town of Thousand Palms. Photograph taken May 1, 2006.

Deep Canyons

Ladder Canyon, a tributary of Painted Canyon, near the town of Mecca. Photograph taken January 1, 2012.

For better or worse, the scenic splendor of the Coachella Valley is primarily the result of the formation of the San Andreas Fault twenty million years ago. The rising of the steepest escarpment in the continental U.S., the dropping of the largest region below sea level in the Western Hemisphere and the splendid series of palm oases that grow along the fault combine to form unique scenic experiences.

Of course there is a more sinister quality to the San Andreas Fault. The land occasionally moves in opposite directions along the fault. When it does, we feel the movement as an earthquake. This happens almost daily but most of the time these tiny earth tremblers go unnoticed, detected only by the most sensitive seismographs. Land shaking sufficient to be detected by humans is experienced a few times each year. Only once or twice each decade is the earth movement sufficient to frighten residents and cause minor damage. Gigantic earthquakes, the kind that result in major damage to structures, occur every few centuries. Geologists say we are overdue for a very destructive quake.

One of the best areas to view what happens to rock along the San Andreas Fault is in the Mecca Hills (Painted Canyon) and the east end of the Indio Hills. At these locations horizontal rock layers have been bent, ripped apart and tilted on end.

Rocks tilted on end, Painted Canyon at the San Andreas Fault. Photograph taken January, 1987.

Canyons represent fractures or faults in rock. Over eons of time, the broken material along the fracture is washed away creating a canyon. Both precipitation and runoff bring water to canyons and most canyons have less evaporation because their bottoms are shaded much of the day. Greater moisture availability results in more plant life unless the canyon is narrow and regularly scoured by floodwaters.

Many plant and animal species are found only in canyon environments. The California treefrog (*Hyla cadaverina*) is a canyon specialist as is the banded rock lizard (*Streptosaurus mearnsi*). Wildflower species closely associated with local canyon environments include California fuchsia (*Epilobium canum*), desert tobacco (*Nicotiana clevelandii*), Emory's rock daisy (*Perityle emoryi*), ghost flower (*Mohavea confertiflora*) and Mecca aster (*Xylorhiza cognata*).

Dozens of canyons surrounding the valley are fully accessible and can be hiked at any time. Those located in the Indian Canyons Tribal Park are the most spectacular since they support streams through all or most of the year and have the greatest diversity of plant life.

Banded Rock Lizard, Petrosaurus mearnsi, *a lizard restricted to canyons and rock outcrops on the south edge of the valley.*

Beaver-Tail Cactus, Opuntia basilaris, *in bloom in local canyon. Photograph taken March 18, 2008.*

When we think of desert trees palo verde, ironwood, mesquite, desert willow and smoke tree come to mind. Some may argue these are large shrubs since they have too short a trunk or none at all. But consider the Coachella Valley's western sycamore, *Platanus racemosa.* Even persons with a passing interest in plants know that a sycamore is a tree. Adults have a single trunk, dozens of large branches and a height that can exceed one hundred feet.

To be sure, a sycamore is not adapted to desert conditions. It requires moist, well-drained soil. These conditions are only met in canyons with large drainage areas in the San Jacinto, San Bernardino and western Santa Rosa mountains. The most accessible location where wild western sycamores occur is Andreas Canyon in the Indian Canyons Tribal Park. Sycamores can also be viewed in Chino Canyon on the way to the Palm Springs Aerial Tramway. They occur in the Whitewater Preserve in Whitewater Canyon as well. Thin, light gray to tan outer bark and lighter inner bark plus maple-like leaves distinguish sycamores from other trees.

Sycamores and cottonwoods show their fall colors in Andreas Canyon, Indian Canyons Tribal Park. Photograph taken December 17, 2007.

Western Sycamore, Plantanus racemosa, *in Chino Canyon. Photograph taken November, 1995.*

Brittlebush, Encelia farinosa, *in Whitewater Canyon. Photograph taken April 22, 2010.*

Rattlesnakes in Canyons

Rattlesnakes are most commonly encountered in canyons because this is the habitat most frequented by hikers. The combination of water and relatively dense vegetation also attracts animals, some of which are prey for rattlers.

Unfortunately, all snakes get a bad rap. They are often said to be dangerous, even deadly. Lack of legs makes them "creepy" to some and they are occasionally described as "slimy." Few laypersons have anything positive to say about a snake's appearance. By default, they are ugly creatures. All of these comments, however, are inaccurate.

Myth #1 Snakes are dangerous, even deadly. There are twenty-six snake species living in the Coachella Valley; only five are dangerous. None of the local rattlesnakes can be considered deadly since more than 99% of all victims survive. In fact, though dozens have been bitten there is only one local record of a person dying from a rattler's bite.

Myth #2 Snakes are insignificant components of the natural world. Most snake species, especially rattlesnakes, eat rodents that can eat plants in yards, food in homes and agricultural products. Farmers have been known to pay school boys to catch gopher snakes to be released in agricultural fields to control rodents. Snakes eat more rodents that all other predators combined.

Myth #3 Snakes are ugly, slimy creatures. The scaly skin of snakes feels cool, dry and smooth, never slimy. In one formal experiment twenty adults were interviewed, all of whom claimed to be horrified of snakes. In a controlled environment behind glass, they were shown a live mountain kingsnake, shovel-nosed snake and ring-necked snake— all colorful species found in the area. Nineteen of the people said the snakes were "attractive" if not "beautiful."

Speckled Rattlesnake, Crotalus mitchellii, *resting in a Santa Rosa Mountains canyon.*

Wildfires were once extremely rare in desert regions. Buring chaparral and forest plant communities to the immediate west of the Coachella Valley ran out of fuel when they reached desert hillsides or the valley floor.

This is no longer true. With the arrival of exotic weed species whose dry skeletons persist between desert shrubs throughout the year, fire has an unbroken pathway into the desert. Today, at least one wildfire per year races down into the Coachella Valley and across the desert, sometimes for more than a mile.

Without having to contend with a fire regime, most desert shrubs and cacti have not evolved adaptations to survive the intense heat and flames of a wildfire. Thus, a fire can permanently alter a desert ecosystem, making it even more susceptible to exotic weed invasions. Frequent droughts in the last two decades seem to have exacerbated the phenomenon.

A plane drops chemicals on a wildfire in the Indian Canyons
Tribal Park. Photograph taken September 8, 2011.

Fire near Chino Canyon.
Photograph taken
September 1, 2005.

Mountains that Protect

Arizona lupine, Lupinus arizonicus,
in foothills of San Jacinto Mountains.
Palm Springs and the Santa Rosa
Mountains in the distance.
Photograph taken March 16, 2010.

ount San Jacinto is the scenic anchor of the Coachella Valley. The northeast face rises 10,000 feet in 6.6 miles making it the steepest escarpment in the continental U.S. Its proximity makes it appear to be the tallest peak in the region. At 10,834 feet above sea level, however, San Jacinto Peaks is actually the second highest summit. San Gorgonio Peak, at 11,502 feet is the highest peak in Southern California. The latter peak lies farther away, to the north and west of San Jacinto Peak, and so does not appear as tall from the valley floor.

Both peaks and their respective mountain systems are primarily responsible for the desert conditions that prevail in the Coachella Valley. Most storms come from the west and must pass over the mountains to reach the valley. As they do so, the air cools and water condenses into raindrops or snowflakes. By the time the storm arrives in the valley most of the water has already fallen on the windward (western) slopes.

Palm Springs Aerial Tramway begins at the Valley Station, elevation 2,643 feet above sea level. The Mountain Station, at the end of the tram, is located at an elevation of 8,516 feet.

Mojave yuccas, Yucca schidigera, *in foreground, 10,834 foot Mount San Jacinto in background. Photograph taken March 17, 2008.*

It seems hard to believe that a dense, coniferous forest thrives just a few miles from the Coachella Valley, one of the lowest, hottest and driest regions in North America. Yet at the top of the Palm Springs Aerial Tramway thousands of pine and fir trees exist in an environment characterized by freezing winter temperatures and a snow pack that can be several feet thick. Spring arrives very late above 8,000 feet with mountain wildflowers not becoming abundant until June.

By way of contrast, the desert floor of the Coachella Valley rarely experiences temperatures below freezing and snow has not touched the valley floor for more than forty years. Spring bloom begins in January and vanishes by May.

When July temperatures exceed 110° F. on the valley floor the top of the tram often does not even reach 80 degrees F.

Few places in North America have such remarkable environmental diversity in such close proximity.

A coniferous forest, complete with winter snow, dominates the landscape just a few miles from the desert floor of the Coachella Valley. Photograph taken February, 1996.

The desert agave is one of the most distinctive plants in the Coachella Valley region. It is not, however, a valley plant. Agaves are only found in the Santa Rosa Mountains—on the hillsides, canyon walls and peaks at the valley's southern edge. The most accessible displays are found along Highway 74, south of Palm Desert. Blooming begins in April and persists through late June. The presence of agave indicates summer rain is more probable in the Santa Rosa Mountains than anywhere else in the Coachella Valley region.

The desert woodrat, Neotoma lepida, *often builds its above-ground stick nest in clumps of agave.*

Desert agaves, Agave deserti, *blossoming in the Santa Rosa Mountains at the valley's southern edge. Photograph taken June 8, 2006.*

*Joshua trees (Yucca brevifolia),
in Joshua Tree National Park
overlooking the Coachella Valley.
Photograph taken February 28, 2011.*

Like the Joshua tree of the Mojave, the ocotillo is an iconic plant of the Sonoran Desert. Unlike the desert agave that is limited in its distribution to hills and slopes of the Santa Rosa Mountains, the ocotillo is much more widespread in the Coachella Valley region. Not only is it found on the lower third of the Santa Rosa Mountains, it also occurs on the alluvial fans and bajadas of the eastern Coachella Valley all the way to the Chihuahuan Desert in Texas.

More than most plants, the ocotillo's appearance is closely tied to environmental conditions. Gradually shortening nights in spring stimulate the best flowering. Each stem tip becomes adorned with bright reddish-orange flowers beginning in March. The appearance of leaf-covered stems is dependent upon rainfall. The ocotillo is drought deciduous, meaning that it produces leaves only after it rains.

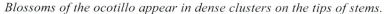

Blossoms of the ocotillo appear in dense clusters on the tips of stems.

Fog bound ocotillos in leaf, Santa Rosa and San Jacinto Mountains National Monument. Photograph taken January 5, 2008.

On lower desert mountainsides and bajadas lives a small, frisky mammal that visitors often mistake for a chipmunk. Known as the white-tailed antelope squirrel, *Ammospermophilus leucurus,* it is distinguished from a chipmunk by the lack of white stripes on its face.

 The antelope squirrel is often the only mammal observed in an entire day of hiking. Typically, it is first seen while rapidly flicking its conspicuous white tail. As the squirrel bounds from one boulder to the next, it is reminiscent of a ping-pong ball bouncing among the rocks.

Blossoms and buds of the golden cholla, Cylindropuntia echinocarpa, *are favorite foods of antelope squirrels.*

Antelope squirrels can become quite tame around homes located next to the hillside habitat of the squirrel.

The California barrel cactus, *Ferocactus cylindraceus*, is the largest and one of the most widespread cacti in the region. It is found on all bajadas, alluvial fans and mountainsides around the Coachella Valley.

Old motion pictures and television programs have made barrel cacti famous for providing life-saving water to lost and weary travelers. The interior of the barrel cactus is remarkably juicy and the liquid can be consumed. Yet a chemical evaluation of the fluid indicates it is too alkaline to drink. In fact, a dehydrated person would be worse off after drinking the juice.

In past times, barrel cacti were collected, prepared and eaten by Native Americans. All products of the plant's reproductive cycle were consumed providing a harvest that lasted several months. In March, April and May Indian women collected the buds and flowers. In June and July the ripened fruits were harvested. Plant parts were plucked from the top of the cactus with two sticks to avoid sharp spines. Buds, flowers or fruits were then parboiled to remove bitterness. The harvested parts were eaten after cooking or dried in the sun and stored.

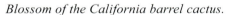

Blossom of the California barrel cactus.

Competing barrel cactus and desert agave,
Santa Rosa Mountains in distance.
Photograph taken June, 14, 2007.

97

Two or three times a decade Coachella Valley hillsides turn yellow with massive flowering of brittlebush. The shift from drab tans and browns to brilliant yellow escapes the attention of few and is a clear sign spring has arrived.

For about six months brittlebush lies dormant and appears dead with no leaves and dry, brittle stems (the characteristic from which its common name is derived). Plant physiologists say it is drought deciduous because it drops its leaves not in response to cold temperatures in fall but in response to drying out of the soil. Since it is primarily the leaves of a plant that use water for photosynthesis and pass water into the air during transpiration, shedding leaves is an excellent way to conserve moisture. The downside of this adaptation is an individual shrub cannot grow larger or reproduce while it is leafless and dormant. Cycles of leaf growth and leaf shedding occur after heavy rainfall and can happen at least three times a year.

Flowers of the Brittlebush, Encelia farinosa.

*Brittlebush in bloom on the lower
slopes of the Santa Rosa Mountains.
Photograph taken April 2, 2010.*

Sub-alpine forest near San Jacinto Peak, view to northwest towards Desert Hot Springs.

One is not likely to forget the glimpse of a wild bighorn. Seen on a precipitous cliff, the muscular torso and massive horns of an adult ram is a scene befitting any postcard. It is also a scene usually reserved for the adventurous hiker who climbs deep into desert ranges in search of the elusive species.

Bighorn sheep generally vacate areas of human activity, preferring an isolated existence removed from humankind. Open terrain with broad vistas and steep, boulder-strewn slopes are preferred habitat. In such areas they are found from hillsides of only a few hundred feet to several thousand feet in all of the mountains surrounding the Coachella Valley. Bighorn are closely tied to desert waterholes, particularly in summer. The dry forage they consume contains little moisture. Hot temperatures force them to evaporate precious body water to keep from overheating. These two factors combine to create a body water deficit that can only be repaid by drinking.

Bighorn ram (male) at the Living Desert, Palm Desert.

A ewe (female) and her lamb, Boyd Deep Canyon Desert Research Center, Palm Desert. Photograph taken May 12, 2005.

Peaks of the San Jacinto Mountains are tall enough to capture rainfall throughout the year. A small fraction of the runoff makes its way into perennial stream courses and a fraction of the stream water is captured in small dams in Snow Creek, Falls Creek and Chino Canyon.

The dammed water is funneled into the Desert Water Agency's domestic water supply that serves Palm Springs and surrounding communities in the upper Coachella Valley. Though the overwhelming majority of domestic water in the Coachella Valley comes from groundwater via wells, approximately 5% of Desert Water Agency's annual supply comes from the three streams emanating from the San Jacinto Mountains.

Tahquitz Canyon Stream is one of several perennial water courses that drain the San Jacinto Mountains.

California Barrel Cactus and Mount San Jacinto. Photograph taken April 26, 2010.

Two Deserts

The Coachella Valley is bounded on the north by the Little San Bernardino Mountains, Mojave Desert and Joshua Tree National Park. Because the Coachella Valley, indeed all of the Sonoran Desert of southeastern California, averages less than one thousand feet in elevation it is locally referred to as the "Low Desert."

The Mojave Desert (which encompasses the nearby communities of Morongo Valley, Yucca Valley, Joshua Tree and Twentynine Palms) is referred to as the "High Desert" because average elevations exceed two thousand feet above sea level. Joshua trees (*Yucca brevifolia*), as shown in the background of the photograph to the right, are indicative of the Mojave Desert.

Whereas the Coachella Valley rarely records winter temperatures below freezing, the adjacent Mojave Desert often experiences below freezing temperatures on winter nights.

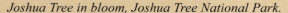

Joshua Tree in bloom, Joshua Tree National Park.

Mount San Jacinto from Morongo Valley in the Mojave Desert. Plant in foreground is calico cactus. Photograph taken May 3, 2010.

Salton Sea, Largest Lake

Snowy Egret, Egretta thula

The Whitewater River brings freshwater into the north end of the Salton Sea. Santa Rosa Mountains in background. Photograph taken February, 1990.

Shoreline of the Salton Sea near
Salton Sea State Recreation Area.
Photograph taken January 2, 2012.

The Salton Trough is a large basin that has dropped below sea level as a result of earth movements along the San Andreas Fault. The basin is the most extensive area of below-sea-level land in the Western Hemisphere. The basin includes a large portion of central Riverside County as well as the western half of Imperial County.

Over the past half million years the course of the Colorado River has alternately flowed into the Salton Trough and then changed course into the Gulf of California. Sediment buildup in the heavily silt laden Colorado River is the primary reason for the successive changes in the course of the river. At the time Spanish explorers arrived in the region in the late eighteenth century, the Salton Trough was an enormous dry lake—a giant salt flat.

_____

Canada goose, Branta canadensis, *on pond near Salton Sea.*

Salt flat along the west shore of the Salton Sea. Photograph taken January 12, 2012.

*Late afternoon on the northeast
shore of the Salton Sea.
Photograph taken April, 2006*

The Salton Sea we know today was created by accident in 1905. An ill-conceived irrigation project failed to take into account high spring runoff levels and the entire Colorado River ran through a manmade irrigation breach in the riverbank. For two years the river ran unchecked into the below-sea-level Salton Trough. Runoff irrigation water maintains the level of the lake today.

The Salton Sea region is famous for the number and diversity of birds it attracts, particularly in winter. More than four hundred species have been observed with total numbers in the millions. Because aquatic environments are diminishing rapidly in the American Southwest, the Salton Sea is one of the last great inland water habitats.

———————————————————————————

Black-necked stilt, Himantopus mexicanus.

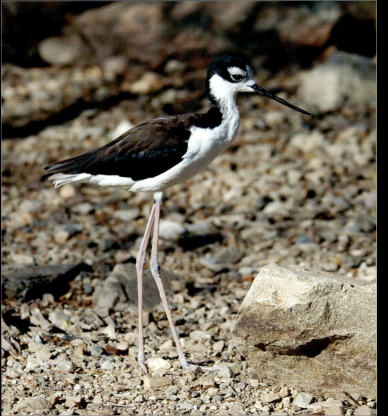

Great egret, Ardea alba, *is common around the Salton Sea.*

Cahuilla Legacy

Petroglyphs at the base of the Santa Rosa Mountains, south of Martinez Canyon. Photograph taken December 31, 2011.

There were people living in the Coachella Valley when European explorers entered the region in the late 18th century. These first residents had been present for at least three thousand years. They were gathering and storing mesquite pods, fishing at the shoreline of an enormous ancient lake and hunting deer and bighorn sheep in the mountains surrounding the valley.

These first people are known as the Cahuilla, pronounced Ka-wee'-yah. Linguistic analysis suggests the Cahuilla are most closely related to the Aztecs of Mexico and the Hopi and Pima of Arizona. Cahuilla language and cultural traditions were practiced by the people who lived in what is today western Riverside County and southern San Bernardino County, California, an area of about 3,500 square miles.

Cahuilla people are alive and well today. Much of the Coachella Valley is reservation land managed by the Cahuilla to protect their natural resources as well as establish a variety of economic enterprises.

A semi-portable rock mortar and pestle used to grind seeds.

Mortar in large boulder, Palm Canyon, Indian Canyons Tribal Park. Mortar contained mesquite pods and other fruits and seeds while ground and pounded into flour. At first there was a slight depression in the rock. However, after hundreds of years of pounding with stone pestles, a deep hole was created. Photograph taken January, 2006.

The Fish Traps at Jackson Street and 66th Avenue were constructed to lure fish into shallow water along the shore of Ancient Lake Cahuilla. Photograph taken November, 2005.

The Cahuilla Indians maximized the benefits of their often hostile environment through seasonal movements up and down the surrounding mountains. Many families spent the months of summer and fall in the relatively cool, high altitude environments of the San Jacinto and Santa Rosa mountains. In late fall they would return to the valley floor and remain there through spring. Using this strategy they could take advantage of seasonal abundance of plant foods at different elevations.

Palm fruits began ripening in late November and were harvested continually through January. The harvesting of ephemeral seeds, from plants such as chia, could begin in February and continue through April. Mesquite pods were harvested in June, just before a family traveled to the high country for summer. Most mountain plants bloom and produce seed in July. By September nuts of pinyon pine and oak were ready to be gathered.

Ground mesquite pods were important food of the Cahuilla.

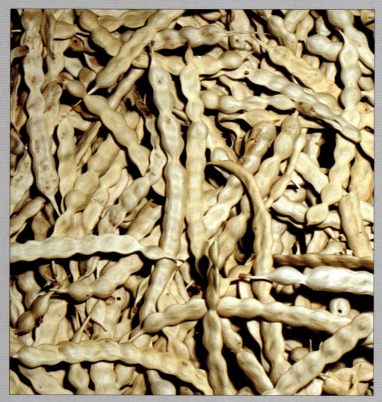

A type of Cahuilla house or "kish" has been recreated in Andreas and Palm Canyons in the Indian Canyons Tribal Park immediately south of downtown Palm Springs.

Cahuilla rock art overlooks the Salton Sea near the base of the Santa Rosa Mountains, December 31, 2011.

Palm Canyon, Indian Canyons Tribal Park, ancestral home of the Cahuilla Indians.